FRANKIE
LIKED TO
SING

Words by JOHN SEVEN
Pictures by JANA CHRISTY

Abrams Books for Young Readers, New York

Frankie didn't act Like other kids:

Frankie was always singing.

Frankie didn't look like the other kids in Hoboken, New Jersey, either. He was scrawny and his mom liked to dress him up fancy. She wanted Frankie to stand out from the crowd. When he was a little kid, she took him to the department store to buy suits and collared shirts and ties.

Other kids would call him names and pick fights with him because of his fancy clothes.

The thing Frankie liked to do most of all was sing loudly, alone in his room. Every day after school, he listened to his hero, Bing Crosby, sing on the radio. The radio was Frankie's best friend. They spent a lot of time together.

Frankie liked to sing for other people, too. Sometimes Frankie sang at his dad's saloon. He would take a break from his homework and climb on top of the piano and sing for the fellows there.

When Frankie sang, arguments stopped. The men clapped and cheered. Some even cried. They tossed nickels at Frankie as a way of saying thank you.

Frankie began to wonder if there were other people he could sing to.

Frankie liked to sing at his mom's parties. When Frankie sang, the old ladies put their hands on their cheeks and dreamed they were young again. When Frankie sang, the old men pushed back their hats just a little and grinned. But he wanted to sing for even more people than could fit into his house.

Frankie liked to sing at school. When Frankie sang, the other kids wouldn't worry about times tables or spelling tests anymore. The teachers would stop Frankie from singing in class, but they could not stop the music in his head. Sometimes the songs burst out of him anyhow. Frankie left school as fast as he could. He was much better at singing than he was at studying.

Frankie liked to sing while he worked in Hoboken. When Frankie sang, the job went faster.

Frankie liked to sing on his front stoop, strum his ukulele, and pretend to perform for the neighborhood. Frankie wanted singing to be his job. How could he get people to pay attention? How could he get them to hear his voice?

Frankie's mom knew everybody in Hoboken. She got Frankie jobs singing at parties, dances, and events all over town. Frankie sang into a big megaphone so the crowd could hear him. But sometimes boys made a game out of tossing pennies into the megaphone.

He decided to buy a microphone, just like the one Bing Crosby had. That was a singer's instrument.

One night, Frankie got to see Bing Crosby perform on a stage. Everyone looked at Bing the way Frankie wanted to be looked at. There was a special connection between Bing and his audience. How did Bing do that? Frankie thought he could fill a bigger theater than Bing did, if he worked hard enough.

Frankie worked so hard at singing that soon there was no one in Hoboken who hadn't heard his voice.

Now Frankie dreamed of something bigger. New York City was just across the river. He knew he had to go there.

In New York City, Frankie took voice lessons and got new ideas by working with other musicians. He became an even better singer. Soon, he got to sing on the radio. The sound of his voice made everyone listening believe that Frankie understood exactly how they were feeling. Frankie's voice was like a reassuring pat on the back.

Thanks to the radio, Frankie's voice reached the ears of band leaders. They asked him to come sing with them! Soon Frankie was filling large theaters—just like Bing Crosby! When Frankie sang, girls screamed with excitement. They cried and trembled and waved their handkerchiefs at him because his singing made them burst with happiness. When Frankie sang, everyone in the room felt like they knew him and he knew them.

Frankie made records of his singing so people could take his voice home with them. Now they could listen to Frankie anytime they wanted to. Frankie's voice made people feel like they could get through hard days and have fun on better ones.

His voice could make a big tough guy cry. And could make a little guy feel big enough to ask a girl to dance.

Frankie was soon singing in movies. He sang in one to convince kids to be nice to each other. That was important to Frankie.

Frankie danced in movies, too.
He even sang and danced on-screen
with Bing Crosby! They had a ball.

Frankie sang all around the world. Although people couldn't always understand his words, his voice made him sound like an old friend. No one felt alone when Frankie sang.

Frankie got all kinds of awards. Some were for his acting. Many were for his singing. He also received awards for just being a good guy.

If you go to Hoboken today, there are pictures of Frankie hanging all over town. His name pops up everywhere you look. All of Hoboken is proud of the kid who loved to sing and never stopped. Frankie's still singing.
Can you hear him?

AUTHOR'S NOTE

Francis Albert Sinatra was born in Hoboken, New Jersey, on December 12, 1915. He was the blue-eyed only child of Italian immigrants. His dad, Marty Sinatra, was a tough guy—a boxer, bar owner, and firefighter. The real boss of the family was Frank Sinatra's mother, Dolly, a spitfire whom everyone in town knew because of her work as a midwife and because of her political connections, which helped her husband find jobs and her son make his name as a singer.

Sinatra was a bit of an outsider in what was a rough neighborhood at the time. His love of music meant he was on a different path from many of the other kids. He dropped out of high school after just forty-seven days and instead worked at the docks, catching hot rivets; piled newspapers on delivery trucks; and plastered walls. Like so many kids disposed to the arts, it took him a long time to figure out how he could turn his passion for singing into a career.

Sinatra became a member of the Hoboken Four, a singing quartet that won a radio talent contest in 1935. That was the first time such a huge audience had heard his voice. By 1939, he was working as a singing waiter at a nightclub called the Rustic Cabin. It was there that he got his big break singing for an orchestra, which led to his job singing with the famous Tommy Dorsey band later the same year. In 1946, Sinatra recorded his first solo album, *The Voice of Frank Sinatra.*

What made Sinatra different from other singers?

It was the gritty honesty of his voice. He made the listener feel that whatever emotion he or she was feeling, good or bad, Sinatra felt it, too. His voice made people feel he understood them. He perfected a singing style that treated his voice like a musical instrument, using special phrasing and breathing techniques influenced by musicians he worked with, especially Tommy Dorsey, band leader and trombone player. Sinatra was very important in popularizing what is called the American Songbook, a collection of songs written between the 1920s and 1950s and made popular by Broadway and Hollywood musicals. Over his life, Sinatra recorded at least sixty studio albums and released numerous singles collections, live-concert recordings, and rarities collections.

Sinatra recorded albums his entire life. Some of his biggest hits, songs like "New York, New York" (which reflected his own hopes and dreams as a young man) and "My Way" (which depicted an older man looking back at his life), were released at a later stage in his career. He remains one of the best-selling musical artists of all time, the recipient of eleven Grammy Awards as well as the Grammy Lifetime Achievement Award.

Sinatra also acted in movies, which increased his popularity as a musician. At the end of World War II, he starred in a short film called *The House I Live In*, which served as a statement against racial prejudice. It won an honorary Academy Award in 1946. He won an Academy Award for Best Supporting Actor in the film *From Here to Eternity* in 1953, and he received many other honors, including the Presidential Medal of Freedom. He has three stars on the Hollywood Walk of Fame, and Hoboken's Frank Sinatra Park and Frank Sinatra Post Office are named after him.

Sinatra had quite a few nicknames: *The Voice. Ol' Blue Eyes. The Chairman of the Board.* They all present different sides of him: his talent, his charm, his good looks, his authority. Sinatra would often tell his audiences, "May you live to be one hundred, and may the last voice you hear be mine." This was because he knew that his voice had the power to endure long after his life was over. He was famous for a lot of things, and one of those was his swagger, which means he *knew* he was special and cool. And he was. I saw that swagger twice in my life: once as a twelve-year-old kid in Cincinnati, and the other time with my wife, Jana Christy, in Worcester, Massachusetts. Sinatra did not disappoint. And years after his death, we can all still listen to his voice anytime we want to.

John and Jana's Favorite Frank Sinatra Songs for Young Listeners

The Coffee Song
Come Dance with Me
Fly Me to the Moon
High Hopes
I Got Plenty o' Nuttin'
I've Got the World on a String
Let's Get Away from It All
My Kind of Town
Pocketful of Miracles
River, Stay 'way from My Door
Swinging on a Star
When You're Smiling

BIBLIOGRAPHY

Kaplan, James. *Frank: The Voice.* New York: Doubleday, 2010.
Pignone, Charles. *Frank Sinatra: The Family Album.* New York: Little, Brown, 2007.
Sinatra, Nancy. *Frank Sinatra: An American Legend.* Santa Monica, Calif.: General Pub. Group, 1995.

May you live to be one hundred, and may the last voice you hear be mine.

Library of Congress Cataloging-in-Publication Data

Seven, John.
Frankie liked to sing/by John Seven ; illustrated by Jana Christy.
pages cm
Includes bibliographical references.
ISBN 978-1-4197-1644-7
1. Sinatra, Frank, 1915–1998—Juvenile literature.
2. Singers—United States—Biography—Juvenile literature.
I. Christy, Jana, illustrator. II. Title.
ML3930.S58S48 2015
782.42164092—dc23
[B]
2014041015

Text copyright © 2015 John Seven
Illustrations copyright © 2015 Jana Christy
Book design by Alyssa Nassner
Photo of Frank Sinatra courtesy of Crollalanza/REXUSA

Printed and bound in China
10 9 8 7 6 5 4 3 2 1

Abrams Books for Young Readers are available at special discounts when purchased in quantity
for premiums and promotions as well as fundraising or educational use. Special editions can also be
created to specification. For details, contact special sales@abramsbooks.com or the address below.

ABRAMS
THE ART OF BOOKS SINCE 1949
115 West 18th Street
New York, NY 10011
www.abramsbooks.com

For Andy and Erin.
We'll always have Hoboken. XOXO.

— JS & JC

Special thanks to Frank Sinatra
Enterprises for the use of the album
covers featured here, and especially to
Tina Sinatra for all her support.

FRANK SiNATRA

FRANK SiNATRA DRive